BLACK AMERICANS OF DISTINCTION

IMPORTANT BLACK AMERICANS IN
Arts and Culture

Stuart A. Kallen

ReferencePoint
Press®

San Diego, CA

© 2023 ReferencePoint Press, Inc.
Printed in the United States

For more information, contact:
ReferencePoint Press, Inc.
PO Box 27779
San Diego, CA 92198
www.ReferencePointPress.com

LIBRARY OF CONGRESS CATALOGING-IN-PUBLICATION DATA

Names: Kallen, Stuart A., 1955- author.
Title: Important Black Americans in arts and culture / by Stuart A. Kallen.
Description: San Diego, CA : ReferencePoint Press, Inc., 2023. | Series: Black Americans of distinction | Includes bibliographical references and index.
Identifiers: LCCN 2021047544 (print) | LCCN 2021047545 (ebook) | ISBN 9781678202828 (library binding) | ISBN 9781678202835 (ebook)
Subjects: LCSH: African Americans--Biography--Juvenile literature. | African American entertainers--Biography--Juvenile literature. | African Americans in the performing arts--Juvenile literature. | African Americans in popular culture--Juvenile literature.
Classification: LCC E185.96 .K34 2023 (print) | LCC E185.96 (ebook) | DDC 920.0092/96073--dc23/eng/20211018
LC record available at https://lccn.loc.gov/2021047544
LC ebook record available at https://lccn.loc.gov/2021047545

CONTENTS

The Black Roots of American Culture

The thread of modern Black culture in the United States winds back hundreds of years across thousands of miles. Humanity can trace its roots to Africa, and the people of that vast continent created art, music, poetry, and epic legends that influenced countless societies that followed. Millions of Africans were forced into slavery beginning in the seventeenth century. But African culture was carried to the Americas in the holds of slave ships by surviving shamans, musicians, dancers, poets, and artists.

Ancient African culture was kept alive for centuries in the new lands, passed down from generation to generation. In America, the old mixed with the new, creating vibrant—and uniquely American—forms of expression in music, storytelling, the visual arts, and other outlets. By the early 1900s, Black musicians in New Orleans were creating a new kind of music called jazz that proved to be a powerful force of cultural change. Jazz melded complex African rhythms with the musical styles created by Black Americans, which included work songs, spirituals, and blues. European-style military marching band instruments were added to the mix. By the 1920s, this Black American music style was so popular throughout American society that the decade was known as the Jazz Age. In 1925 Black music critic J.A. Rogers described the cultural influences of jazz music: "Jazz has come to stay because it is an expression of the times, of the breathless, energetic, superactive times in which we are living. . . . The Negro musicians of America are playing a great part in this change. . . . They are not hampered by conventions or traditions, and with their new ideas, their constant experiment, they are causing new blood to flow in the veins of music."[1]

Jive Talk to Hip-Hop

A legacy of slavery, violent and systemic racism continued to dominate the daily lives of most Black Americans even as their cultural contributions fused with American life. But the Jazz Age proved the contributions could not be ignored. The records made by jazz trumpeter Louis Armstrong helped launch the Jazz Age while making him one of the first Black international stars. Armstrong and other jazz musicians, including Duke Ellington and Ella Fitzgerald, broke down racial barriers in the entertainment industry, appearing in top Hollywood movies and playing in fancy clubs that catered to White audiences in big cities across the globe.

> "[Black jazz musicians] are not hampered by conventions or traditions, and with their new ideas, their constant experiment, they are causing new blood to flow in the veins of music."[1]
>
> —J.A. Rogers, music critic

Jazz music inspired international dance crazes, including the Lindy Hop, the Charleston, and the Jitterbug, that originated in Black music clubs. Jazz also spawned a new lexicon that quickly made its way into popular culture. The word *jazz* and other terms, such as *jive, boogie-woogie, hype, hip,* and *riff,* originated in the Black community. There were so many new slang words coming from the Black jazz community that the renowned bandleader Cab Calloway published *Cab Calloway's Hepster's Dictionary* in 1938. This first Black slang dictionary was a best seller. Calloway remarked in the sixth edition in 1944, "'Jive talk' is now an everyday part of the English language. Its usage is now accepted in the movies, on the stage, and in the [most popular songs]. It is reasonable

5

to assume that jive will find new avenues in such hitherto remote places as Australia, the South Pacific, North Africa, China, Italy, France, Sicily, and inevitably Germany."[2]

Calloway died in 1994, but he lived long enough to see his prediction about "jive talk" come true in the form of rap and hip-hop music. Gail Levin, who directed the 2012 *American Masters* documentary "Cab Calloway: Sketches," explains: "It's remarkable . . . how much of an effect he's had on what's modern—hip-hop, rap, street dancing, break dancing . . . one thing after another."[3]

Calloway and Armstrong were among thousands of Black artists who impacted American culture during the era. The Harlem Renaissance, born in the Harlem neighborhood of New York City

Duke Ellington (at the piano) and his renowned band perform in 1945, the year the United States and its allies won World War II. Along with trumpeter Louis Armstrong, Ellington was among several Black entertainers who broke down racial barriers by performing in both major Hollywood films and fancy nightclubs that catered mainly to White audiences.

during the Jazz Age, was another element of Black culture that has since been celebrated as influential beyond its time. The renaissance was a great intellectual awakening led by young Black writers, playwrights, artists, and filmmakers. They provided a unifying voice for millions of Black people who faced segregation and discrimination in the United States. The Harlem Renaissance produced writers such as Zora Neale Hurston and Langston Hughes, who inspired the best-selling Black authors Ralph Ellison, Maya Angelou, Toni Morrison, and Alice Walker in later decades.

Although it lasted little more than a decade, the Jazz Age and the Harlem Renaissance highlighted the important contributions that Black Americans have made to art, society, and culture in America and around the globe. Although these Black cultural movements occurred nearly a century ago, anyone who listens to rock, rhythm and blues (R&B), hip-hop, pop, and even country music can find elements of the Jazz Age in their favorite songs. And today's writers, dancers, and filmmakers continue to find inspiration in the artistic endeavors of Black Americans who made their voices heard in a society that suffered—and continues to suffer—from racial divisions.

CHAPTER ONE

Maya Angelou: Writer and Activist

In 2019, superstar singer Beyoncé released a preview for her Netflix documentary *Homecoming: A Film by Beyoncé*. The short film is composed of video clips of Beyoncé at her 2018 performance at the Coachella Valley Music and Arts Festival. However, the audio track on the trailer does not feature Beyoncé singing. Instead, viewers hear the voice of literary icon Maya Angelou. "What I really want to do is be a representative of my race, of the human race," Angelou intones in her distinctive voice. "I have a chance to show how kind we can be, how intelligent and generous we can be. I have a chance to teach and love and to laugh and I know that when I'm finished doing what I'm sent here to do, I will be called home."[4]

Beyoncé is among millions of adoring fans who have been influenced by Angelou's wisdom, humor, and unique storytelling abilities. Angelou was a poet and the author of seven celebrated memoirs, including *I Know Why the Caged Bird Sings.* In addition to topping bestseller lists, Angelou worked as an actor, director, singer, dancer, composer, screenwriter, civil rights activist, college lecturer, and distinguished visiting professor at several universities. She was granted more than thirty honorary degrees and won dozens of awards, including a Grammy, a Pulitzer Prize, and a National Book Award.

In 2014 Angelou was "called home" at the age of eighty-six. Her death prompted journalist Rachel Nuwer to write, "It's difficult to put a single label on her legacy."[5]

A Traumatic Childhood

When Angelou was a child, few would have imagined that she was destined for greatness. Born Marguerite Annie Johnson in St. Louis, Missouri, in 1928, her early life was marked by disruption, trauma, and abuse. Angelou's mother, Vivian Baxter Johnson, was a card dealer at a local gambling parlor, and her father, Bailey Johnson Sr., worked as a cook. Angelou had a brother, Bailey Jr., who was one year older. He called her "Mya Sister," and everyone soon called her by the nickname "Maya."

Angelou describes her parent's marriage as calamitous; they were divorced when she was three. After the divorce Bailey Sr. sent Angelou and her brother to stay with his mother, Annie Henderson, who owned a general store in the small town of Stamps, Arkansas. Like almost all towns in the southern United States, Stamps was strictly segregated. Black people faced bigotry and racial violence daily. Angelou later wrote that most Black children in Stamps never saw a White person, but they were taught to fear them.

Angelou was seven when she and Bailey Jr. were sent without warning from Stamps to their mother's home in St. Louis. Vivian lived with her boyfriend, a man referred to as Mr. Freeman. When Angelou was eight, Freeman raped her. Angelou confided in her brother, who told the rest of the family. Freeman was arrested and put on trial. Although Angelou was a young child, she was put on the witness stand to testify against Freeman. He was found guilty, but for reasons unknown, he only served one day in jail. Several days after Freeman's release, he was found dead, most likely murdered by Angelou's uncles. The trauma of the incident

> "It's difficult to put a single label on [Angelou's] legacy."[5]
>
> —Rachel Nuwer, journalist

James Baldwin and Maya Angelou

Black activist and author James Baldwin was instrumental in getting Maya Angelou to write her first memoir, *I Know Why the Caged Bird Sings*. And Angelou's inspiration for the book came from Baldwin's first novel, *Go Tell It on the Mountain* (1953). Like *Caged Bird*, the book combines autobiography with elements of fiction.

Baldwin was best known for his essay collection *The Fire Next Time* (1963), which discusses issues of race and racism in stark terms. Baldwin's aim was to reach White audiences and help them understand the struggles of Black people in segregated America. Baldwin succeeded; much like Angelou in later decades, Baldwin was seen as a spokesperson for Black culture and Black civil rights. He was featured in national magazines and invited to speak on television talk shows.

Angelou called Baldwin her "brother friend." When he died in 1987, Angelou wrote in his obituary, "James Baldwin knew that black women in this desolate world, black women in this cruel time which has no soundness in it, have a quiet need for brothers. He knew that a brother's love redeems a sister's pain. His love opened the unusual door for me, and I am blessed that James Baldwin was my brother."

Maya Angelou, "My Brother Jimmy Baldwin," *Los Angeles Times,* December 20, 1987. www.latimes.com.

deeply affected Angelou; she felt that Freeman died because she told her brother about the abuse. Angelou convinced herself that her voice could kill people and refused to speak for five years.

A Love of Poetry

Angelou and Bailey Jr. were sent back to Stamps. While she remained mute, she continued to attend school, where she became a voracious reader. Angelou found a mentor in a wealthy woman named Bertha Flowers, whom she described as "the aristocrat of Black Stamps."[6] Flowers introduced Angelou to classic works by Charles Dickens, William Shakespeare, Edgar Allan Poe, and

Black author and civil rights activist James Weldon Johnson. Flowers also instilled a love of poetry in Angelou by giving her books by Black poets, including Frances Harper and Anne Spencer. During this period, Angelou began writing poetry and essays in personal journals.

Angelou later said that when she stopped speaking, the part of her brain that would have been used for speech had nothing to do. This allowed her to develop an incredible memory. "I memorized 60 Shakespearean sonnets," she said. "And some of the things I memorized, I'd never heard them spoken, so I memorized them according to the cadence that I heard in my head. I loved Edgar Allan Poe and I memorized everything I could find."[7]

Flowers prompted Angelou to read her favorite poems aloud, and by the time she was fourteen, she was speaking again. During this period, Angelou's life changed dramatically. She went to live with her mother, who had moved to San Francisco. Although Angelou rarely had heard from Vivian growing up, she held little resentment toward her mother: "I was an abandoned child as far as I was concerned. . . . My mom was a terrible parent of young children. . . . Ah, but my mother was a great parent of a young adult."[8] Vivian respected Angelou's intelligence and encouraged her to expand her horizons by taking drama and dance classes.

Fighting for Civil Rights

During her last year in high school, Angelou had a short relationship with a neighborhood boy. She got pregnant at age seventeen, and three weeks after graduation gave birth to a son, Guy Johnson. In 1951 she married a Greek musician named Tosh Angelos and moved to New York City. During this period, Angelou studied African dance and worked as a dancer in nightclubs. Angelou's marriage ended in 1954. By this time, she was back in San Francisco singing calypso, a style of rhythmic music that originated in the Caribbean island nation of Trinidad and Tobago. Angelou, who wanted a memorable stage name, legally changed her name to Maya Angelou.

By 1960 Angelou was writing short stories and essays in her spare time. She showed them to novelist John Killens, who encouraged her to move to New York City to join the Harlem Writers Guild. The guild was founded in the late 1940s by Black writers who were excluded from the mainstream publishing industry. Angelou met famed Black writer James Baldwin at the guild, and he encouraged her to pursue a career as an author.

When Angelou arrived in New York, she found a world far different from the less hectic scene she had left behind in San Francisco. Angelou wrote in her memoir *The Heart of a Woman,* "We were living in exciting times . . . [because] oppressed people from all over the world were making New York the arena where they fought for justice."[9] Angelou was referring to people such as American civil rights activist Martin Luther King Jr. and South African leader Oliver Tambo, who was fighting at home against the rigid form of segregation known as apartheid. These leaders were supported by a wide range of Black authors, actors, and political activists, including Angelou. She took a leadership role in organizing protest rallies, sit-ins, and political fund-raisers for the cause.

In 1961 Angelou became romantically involved with a South African anti-apartheid activist named Vusumzi Make. Angelou and Guy moved with Make to Cairo, Egypt, but the relationship with Make soon ended. Angelou worked for a time in Cairo as an editorial assistant at the English-language magazine *Arab Observer.* In 1963 she moved to Accra, Ghana, where Guy enrolled in the University of Ghana. During her travels, Angelou became fluent in Arabic, Spanish, French, Italian, and Fanti, a West African language.

Putting Feelings into Words

Angelou met civil rights leader Malcolm X while in Ghana. They worked together to develop the Organization of Afro-American Unity, an international group meant to link American and African civil rights activists. The group never met, however. Malcolm X was assassinated in New York in May 1965, just two days after Angelou moved back to the United States. Angelou was devastated by the news, but it strengthened her resolve to remain active in the civil rights movement.

In early 1968 Angelou agreed to help Martin Luther King Jr. organize a civil rights march in New York City. Sadly, like three years before, the event never took place. King was assassinated on April 4, 1968, which was Angelou's fortieth birthday. For many years after the tragedy, Angelou refused to celebrate her birthday, spending the day instead mourning the loss with King's widow, Coretta Scott King.

Maya Angelou poses with a copy of her best-selling memoir I Know Why the Caged Bird Sings. *Over the course of decades, she demonstrated her abilities not only as a best-selling writer and poet, but also as a singer, dancer, actress, director, screenwriter, civil rights activist, and highly respected college lecturer.*

After the assassination Angelou tried to lift her spirits by attending a dinner hosted by popular cartoonist Jules Feiffer and his wife, Judy. The celebrities who attended took turns telling stories from their childhoods. Angelou spoke about her life in Stamps, which deeply impressed Judy. She called an editor she knew at Random House publishing, Robert Loomis, and told him to convince Angelou to write a book. Angelou, who thought of herself as a poet, refused. Upon the advice of Baldwin, Loomis used reverse psychology to persuade Angelou. As she tells it, "[He said,] 'it's just as well, because to write an autobiography as literature is just about impossible.'"[10] Angelou took this as a challenge and decided to write *I Know Why the Caged Bird Sings.* The book details Angelou's life up to age eighteen. It is written in a unique style that mixes factual information with fictional elements like made-up dialog. This blend led reviewers to call *I Know Why the Caged Bird Sings* a work of autobiographical fiction.

When *I Know Why the Caged Bird Sings* was published in 1969, few people cared about the book's specific genre. Angelou's unflinching themes focused on poverty, racism, rape, and other painful issues that struck a chord with the reading public. *I Know Why the Caged Bird Sings* was nominated for a National Book Award in 1970 and has never been out of print.

> "I bonded with [Angelou's] every word. Every page revealed insights and feelings I had never been able to articulate."[11]
>
> —Oprah Winfrey, talk show host

Angelou was described as an influential new voice who spoke for all Black girls and women. This sentiment was echoed by television talk show host Oprah Winfrey, who, similar to Angelou, grew up in Mississippi and was molested by several family members when she was nine. Winfrey, who was fifteen when *I Know Why the Caged Bird Sings* was published, was awestruck that she and Angelou shared the same feelings, longings, and perceptions. As Winfrey wrote in 2015, "I was that girl who loved to read. I was that girl raised by my Southern grandmother. I was the girl raped at nine, who muted the telling of it. . . . I bonded with her every word. Every page revealed insights and feelings I had never been able to articulate."[11]

Poetry for the People

The success of *I Know Why the Caged Bird Sings* raised Angelou's profile considerably, and her talents were in high demand. During the early 1970s she wrote a screenplay, a film soundtrack, and composed songs with singer Roberta Flack. Angelou also focused on writing her second autobiography, *Gather Together in My Name*. Released to great acclaim in 1974, the memoir covers Angelou's life from ages seventeen through nineteen. Two years later Angelou published *Singin' and Swingin' and Gettin' Merry like Christmas*. In this book, Angelou frankly addresses the problems she faced as a young, single mother in her early twenties. *The Heart of a Woman* (1981) covers Angelou's life between 1957 and 1962. In her fifth autobiography, *All God's Children Need Traveling Shoes* (1986), Angelou discusses her life in Ghana.

Angelou remained an inspiration and best-selling author for decades. But she became an international celebrity in January 1993 when President Bill Clinton asked her to recite a poem at his first inauguration. When Angelou read the piece she had written, "On the Pulse of Morning," she connected with people of all races, nationalities, and backgrounds. A week after the inauguration, all five volumes of Angelou's memoirs returned to best-seller lists, with total sales increasing up to 600 percent from the previous year. The recording of Angelou reading "On the Pulse of Morning" won the 1994 Grammy Award for Best Spoken Word Album.

Fame and Influence

After Angelou's appearance at the inauguration, she said she began receiving the type of adoration from awestruck fans usually reserved for movie stars. "I think my delivery (at the inauguration) had its own impact," she noted. "Before, I could pass 100 people

In January 2021, Amanda Gorman recited her poem "The Hill We Climb" at the presidential inauguration of Joseph R. Biden. At age twenty-three, Gorman was the youngest inaugural poet in history. Gorman's emotional reading of her visionary poem made her an instant literary superstar. She appeared on the cover of *Time* magazine, read another of her poems at the 2021 Super Bowl, and became a best-selling author when "The Hill We Climb" was published.

When Gorman was interviewed in 2021 by Oprah Winfrey, she said Maya Angelou was one of her major inspirations. Gorman said she grounded herself every day by listening to Angelou's 1993 inaugural poem "On the Pulse of Morning." Gorman grew up with a speech impediment. She said she related to Angelou's decision to not speak for many years after she was raped:

> It was an amazing discovery when I was reading "I Know Why the Caged Bird Sings" her autobiography and reading about (Angelou's) issues with speech. . . . I was like "I'm a Black girl with a speech impediment and . . . this great orator that I'm reading had a similar struggle?" Being able to connect with her and relate with that was a real beacon for me in my life.

Quoted in Elise Brisco, "Amanda Gorman Tells Oprah About Her Connection to Maya Angelou: 'It Was an Amazing Discovery,'" *USA Today*, March 26, 2021. www.usatoday.com.

and maybe 10 would recognize me. Now, maybe 40 recognize me. If they hear my voice, another 30 . . . do too."[12]

By the time Angelou's sixth memoir, *A Song Flung Up to Heaven*, was released in 2002, she was widely recognized as the leading Black female voice of her generation. Angelou was also an icon. Fans lined up around the block at her book signings, and her poetry readings in auditoriums often attracted more than three thousand people. Angelou's face appeared on a dizzying array of merchandise, including bookends, pillows, coffee mugs, and posters. She also composed poems for a popular line of greeting cards.

Angelou published one more memoir at age eighty-five, *Mom & Me & Mom* (2013), which featured recollections of her mother. Over the years she also published ten poetry collections and eight books featuring single poems. When she died in 2014, she was working on another memoir about her relations with the national and world leaders she had met over the years. Some of these leaders were joined by celebrated writers, musicians, actors, and everyday people who offered an outpouring of respect and condolences upon Angelou's death.

The list of people who say they were inspired by Angelou's words and actions would fill volumes. They include South African activist Nelson Mandela; rappers Tupac Shakur and Kendrick Lamar; singers Rihanna, Beyoncé, and Nicki Minaj; tennis star Serena Williams; and former president Barack Obama. Angelou was also the leading inspiration to Amanda Gorman, a young poet who delivered "The Hill We Climb" at the presidential inauguration of Joseph R. Biden in January 2021.

Angelou's accomplishments in the face of tragedy and trauma were astounding, but as she said in 2003, she was able to find peace and inspiration in simple words: "Every person in the world . . . uses words. I know of no other art form that we always use. So the writer has to take the most used, most familiar objects—nouns, pronouns, verbs, adverbs—ball them together and make them bounce, turn them a certain way and make people get into a romantic mood; and another way, into a bellicose mood. I'm most happy to be a writer."[13]

CHAPTER TWO

Aretha Franklin: Soul Singer

In the summer of 1967, the song "Respect" by Aretha Franklin was topping the charts and booming out of millions of radios from Los Angeles to London. The hit song made Franklin the hottest new Black voice on the international stage. "Respect" was released at a time when Black activists and feminists were demanding an equal place in society. Franklin later explained why the song touched a collective nerve: "So many people identified with and related to 'Respect.' It was the need of a nation, the need of the average man and woman in the street, the businessman, the mother, the fireman, the teacher—everyone wanted respect. It was also one of the battle cries of the civil rights movement. The song took on monumental significance."[14]

"Respect" was written by superstar soul singer Otis Redding. But Franklin made the song her own with the help of her sisters, Emma and Carolyn Franklin, who arranged and sang the memorable backup vocals on the record. Franklin's version of "Respect" topped the Billboard Hot 100 chart, the Billboard R&B chart, and reached number ten in the United Kingdom. This success made Franklin an international superstar and earned her the title "the Queen of Soul." In 1967 Franklin won a Grammy for the best R&B recording. She also won a Grammy for a new category, the best R&B solo vocal performance by a female. This award was later nicknamed the "Aretha Award" because she went on to win it eight times in a row.

"Respect" is one of the most empowering soul music anthems in music history. And no one could sing it like Franklin, whose vocal range extended to more than three octaves. As music journalist Rob Sheffield writes, "[Whatever] style she was singing, she created that sense of raw intimacy—the toughest and truest of American voices. . . . Aretha made some of pop's most emotionally cathartic music—there's no treatment for heartbreak like a long night spent with [her albums]."[15]

> "Aretha made some of pop's most emotionally cathartic music— there's no treatment for heartbreak like a long night spent with [her albums]."[15]
>
> —Rob Sheffield, music journalist

The Queen of Soul's stirring vocals and successful career inspired Whitney Houston, Mariah Carey, Alicia Keys, Kelly Clarkson, Jennifer Hudson, H.E.R., and countless other singers in the music business. But the woman with the emotionally charged voice who brought joy to so many was not the powerhouse she seemed to be on stage. Franklin was extremely shy. She carried emotional scars from her childhood, had relationships with men who did not respect her, and sometimes struggled with depression. Record producer Jerry Wexler referred to Franklin as "the mysterious lady of sorrow."[16]

At Home in the Church

Aretha Louise Franklin was born in March 1942 in Memphis, Tennessee. Her mother, Barbara Siggers Franklin, was a pianist and a gifted gospel singer. Her father, Clarence LaVaughn "C.L." Franklin, was Baptist minister famous for the thundering sermons he gave in Black churches across the country. As civil rights leader Jesse Jackson explains, "[C.L.] infused his messages with great poetry and startling metaphors. . . . C.L. preached the say-it-loud-I'm-black-and-I'm-proud message . . . [and was] a beacon of strength and hope for the millions."[17] Parishioners donated thousands of dollars to C.L. at each appearance, earning him the nickname "the Man with the Million-Dollar Voice."

When Franklin was five years old, her family settled in Detroit, Michigan, where C.L. served as pastor of the New Bethel Baptist Church. C.L.'s famed sermons attracted Black luminaries to the family home, including actors, authors, musicians, politicians, and activists. However, C.L. had a violent temper and was unfaithful to Barbara. Their marriage dissolved in 1948 when Franklin was six. Barbara moved to Buffalo, New York, without her children. Carolyn Franklin later recalled that Aretha was very close to her mother and would often cry for days after she left. Barbara died of a heart attack in 1952, an unexpected tragedy that traumatized Franklin, who refused to speak for weeks. Family members say Franklin crawled into a shell and remained there for years. What brought her out was the music.

A Child Prodigy

Franklin found her true home in the New Bethel Baptist Church, where she was drawn to the gospel music that nourished her natural talents. Soul superstar Smokey Robinson, who was a family friend, was amazed by Franklin's piano playing. "Even as a seven-year-old, she started playing chords—big chords [on the piano]," he said. "Later I'd recognize them as complex church chords, the kind used to accompany the preacher and the solo singer. . . . Aretha came out of this world, but she also came out of another far-off magical world none of us really understood. She came from a distant musical planet where children are born with their gifts fully formed."[18]

> "[Aretha] came from a distant musical planet where children are born with their gifts fully formed."[18]
>
> —Smokey Robinson, soul singer

At age ten, Franklin sang her first solos in front of several thousand worshippers at New Bethel Baptist Church. Those who knew Franklin say she poured out the emotional loss of

Aretha Franklin was never afraid to express her political views, especially on race and racism. She was a vocal supporter of the civil rights movement, performed at benefits, and encouraged voter registration at her concerts. In 1970 Franklin generated controversy when she offered support to California college professor Angela Davis, a Black power activist and member of the Communist Party. Davis had been arrested for purchasing guns later used by Black prisoners in an escape attempt from a San Rafael courtroom. Several people were killed, including a judge. Although President Richard Nixon called Davis a dangerous terrorist, Franklin offered to post her bail. Franklin made this statement to the press:

> Angela Davis must go free. Black people will be free. . . . I know you got to disturb the peace when you can't get no peace. Jail is hell to be in. I'm going to see her free if there is any justice in our courts, not because I believe in communism, but because she's a Black woman and she wants freedom for Black people. I have the money; I got it from Black people—they've made me financially able to have it—and I want to use it in ways that will help our people.

Quoted in David Ritz, *Respect: The Life of Aretha Franklin*. New York: Little, Brown, 2014, pp. 483–84.

her mother in song. On any given Sunday, Franklin's audience might include gospel star Mahalia Jackson, civil rights leader Martin Luther King Jr., blues pioneer B.B. King, and singers Sam Cooke and Ray Charles. C.L. often hosted parties for his famous friends and would awaken Franklin in the middle of the night to sing for them.

By the time Franklin was twelve, C.L. was taking her on the road as a warm-up act in what he called his traveling religious service. Franklin was thrilled to be part of the exciting itinerate gospel scene, in which she was viewed as a child prodigy. Her singing was often favorably compared to her father's preaching. Those who knew her say the fame helped Franklin leap from childhood to adulthood overnight. Two months before her thirteenth birthday, Franklin gave birth to a baby boy named Clarence. The father was a local boy whom Franklin had met at the roller rink. After having the baby, Franklin was back on the road with her father. And she continued to attend school, where she was an excellent student. After Franklin had a second child, Edward, at age fifteen, she dropped out of school.

Slow Record Sales

In 1957 a new song came out that highlighted the appeal of Black singers who performed gospel music. Sam Cooke's smooth and

Singer and iconic entertainer Aretha Franklin performs in 1968. The year before, her song "Respect" reached number one on both the R&B and pop charts. Dubbed "the Queen of Soul," Franklin later said that the song was based on the fervent desire of all African Americans to be treated with simple decency.

sensuous "You Send Me" sold over 1.7 million copies, spent six weeks at number one on the rhythm and blues (R&B) charts, and crossed over to the top 10 pop charts, where it stayed for three weeks. Before "You Send Me" was recorded, Cooke had spent seven years as the lead singer in the landmark gospel group the Soul Stirrers. The group sang at C.L.'s traveling sermon shows. After the success of "You Send Me," Cooke quit the Soul Stirrers and was instantly transformed into a pop star beloved by teenagers of all races.

Cooke was a family friend, and Franklin quickly recognized his crossover appeal. Like Cooke, she wanted to pursue a career as a pop idol. To prepare for this crossover success, Franklin began closely studying the singing styles of Black jazz singers such as Ella Fitzgerald, Billie Holiday, and Sarah Vaughan. In 1960, shortly after her eighteenth birthday, Franklin recorded a two-song demo, or demonstration record. When Columbia Records executive John H. Hammond heard the demo, he immediately signed Franklin to the record label. Around this time, Franklin married her first husband, Ted White, who began to manage her career. They would later divorce in 1969.

Franklin's first Columbia single, "Today I Sing the Blues," reached number ten on the R&B charts. The song was included on Franklin's first album, *Aretha*, which features a mix of jazz, R&B, Broadway tunes, and standards like "Over the Rainbow." Franklin released two more albums the following year, but sales were slow. In 1965 Franklin recorded some soulful pop songs, including "Runnin' Out of Fools" and "One Step Ahead," which reached the top ten on the R&B charts. The record sales, combined with her concert appearances, helped Franklin earn $100,000 in 1965, a large sum for that era.

Massive Respect

In 1966 Jerry Wexler convinced Franklin to sign with his label, Atlantic Records. The following year Wexler produced three top-ten

In 2015 Aretha Franklin performed an awe-inspiring version of "(You Make Me Feel) Like a Natural Woman" at the Kennedy Center Honors. Many in the audience were moved to tears by the performance, including President Barack Obama, who later commented on Franklin's contribution to music and culture:

> Nobody embodies more fully the connection between the African-American spiritual, the blues, R. & B., rock and roll— the way that hardship and sorrow were transformed into something full of beauty and vitality and hope. American history wells up when Aretha sings. That's why, when she sits down at a piano and sings "A Natural Woman," she can move me to tears . . . because it captures the fullness of the American experience, the view from the bottom as well as the top, the good and the bad, and the possibility of synthesis, reconciliation, transcendence.

Quoted in David Remnick, "Soul Survivor," *New Yorker,* March 28, 2016. www.newyorker.com.

hits with Franklin: "Respect," "Baby I Love You," and "(You Make Me Feel) Like a Natural Woman." These songs were included on Franklin's first Atlantic album, *I Never Loved a Man the Way I Love You,* which reached number two on the Billboard album chart. When Franklin was asked to compare her new records with those she released at Columbia, she said, "When I went to Atlantic they just sat me down at the piano and let me do my thing. The hits just started coming."[19]

By 1968 Franklin was one of the most successful singers in the United States. She changed her somewhat conservative public image and began wearing flashy sequin-spangled gowns and towering wigs. Two albums released in 1968, *Lady Soul* and *Aretha Now,* cemented Franklin's title as the Queen of Soul. These albums featured hits that are now considered classics, including

"Chain of Fools" and "Think." Franklin earned two Grammys for her work on these albums and appeared on the cover of national magazines such as *Jet* and *Time*.

A Best-Selling Gospel Album

By the early 1970s Franklin was an unstoppable musical force. On her 1972 album, *Amazing Grace*, Franklin reinterpreted the gospel standards she had heard in church as a child. *Amazing Grace* was recorded live over two nights with the choir and band of the New Temple Baptist Missionary Church in Los Angeles. *Amazing Grace* sold more than 2 million copies, making it the biggest-selling album of Franklin's career and the top-selling gospel album of all time. Franklin's younger brother, Cecil, put the album in perspective:

> I see [*Amazing Grace*] as the sacred moment in the life of black people. Think back. We had lost Martin [Luther King Jr.]; we had lost Malcolm [X]. . . . Turmoil, anger, corruption, confusion. We needed reassurance and recommitment. We needed redirection. So when Aretha helped lead us back to God—the only force for good that stays steady in this loveless world—I'd call it historical.[20]

Amazing Grace was the high point for Franklin professionally and personally. She went on to have several hit singles, but the other albums she released in the 1970s failed to top the charts. In 1980 Franklin's career received a considerable boost when she played the owner of a soul food restaurant in the blockbuster comedy film *The Blues Brothers*. The movie appearance helped propel record sales when she released the single "Jump to It" in 1982. The song was Franklin's first top-forty single in six years. By the mid-1980s her albums were once again selling millions of copies. Sheffield concludes, "You could make a case that the Eighties were Aretha's decade. No 1960s star had a better 1980s run. . . . For Eighties . . . kids, Aretha represented pure intensity and integrity, which is why we idolized her. . . . The Queen never needed to make any kind of comeback again—she was firmly established once and for all."[21]

Franklin continued to release critically acclaimed albums for the rest of her life. Her thirty-eighth and final studio album, *Aretha Franklin Sings the Great Diva Classics* (2014), showed that Franklin had never lost her sensational voice. The album debuted at number thirteen on the Billboard 200, selling twenty-three thousand copies in its first week.

Franklin died from pancreatic cancer on August 16, 2018, at the age of seventy-six. Her death triggered an outpouring of tributes from celebrities and political leaders throughout the world. Franklin's Detroit funeral was covered by all the major news networks and attracted luminaries, including Ariana Grande, Jennifer Hudson, Cedric the Entertainer, and Bill Clinton.

For all the money and respect accorded to Franklin, her life was never easy. For most of her life she chain-smoked cigarettes, drank alcohol to excess, and had weight problems. Songwriter Clyde Otis said that Franklin appeared to carry the weight of the world on her shoulders in the 1960s, and he was amazed she could shake off her depression to sing. And as Hammond said, Franklin had "terrible luck"[22] with men. But she never showed her depression to the world and worked to keep her personal life private.

Aretha Franklin never forgot her roots. She was involved in the civil rights movement her entire life. She met civil rights icon Martin Luther King Jr. as a child, worked with him in the 1960s, and sang at his funeral when he was assassinated in 1968. In the early 1970s, Franklin started a charitable foundation for mothers on welfare funded with the proceeds from five concerts a year. In a career marked by highs and lows, the Queen of Soul fought for respect—not only for herself but also for those on the bottom of society's ladder who needed it the most. As African American studies professor Reiland Rabaka put it, "['Respect'] will be relevant as long as there is a lot of disrespect in America."[23] Perhaps noting such recognition, in September 2021, *Rolling Stone* magazine crowned "Respect" as the greatest song of all time.

CHAPTER THREE

Spike Lee: Filmmaker

It was the hottest day of the summer in the Bedford-Stuyvesant neighborhood of Brooklyn, New York. A large Black man nicknamed "Radio" Raheem got into an altercation with a White pizzeria owner. The police arrived and immediately grabbed Raheem. An officer used a nightstick to place Raheem in a choke hold while onlookers screamed out that the man could not breathe. Raheem briefly struggled, his body went limp, and he died. The entire scene was captured on film. But the camera stopped rolling when the director, Spike Lee, yelled to cut. Bill Nunn, an actor playing Raheem, got up from the pavement. The killing was a scene from Lee's 1989 film *Do the Right Thing.*

Raheem's movie death resembled real police killings of Black men in New York at the time and was similar to others that followed. In 2014, Eric Garner, a Black man, was approached by New York City police for illegally selling cigarettes. He was put in a choke hold by a police officer as he kept saying, "I can't breathe."[24] Garner died. In May 2020 a Black man named George Floyd begged for his life as Minneapolis police officer Derek Chauvin knelt on his neck, saying over and over, "I can't breathe"[25] This incident was also filmed, and the teenager who shot the video then uploaded it to social media sites. Floyd's death sparked massive antiracism protests in 550 American cities. Several days after Floyd died, Lee posted a video to Twitter called "3 Brothers—Radio Raheem, Eric Garner and George Floyd." The video, which intercuts Raheem's fictional death with those of Garner and Floyd, starts with the question "When will history stop repeating itself?"[26]

Countless people post mash-ups of current events on Twitter, but when Spike Lee makes a video statement, people pay attention. Lee is the filmmaker behind dozens of award-winning movies and documentaries that focus on urban life, gang violence, police brutality, racial politics, and race relations in America. And although other films might shine a light on these topics, Lee offers a perspective not often seen in typical Hollywood films. Lee grew up in Brooklyn not far from the streets where he filmed 1989's *Do the Right Thing* and several other movies.

An Outspoken Student Filmmaker

Shelton Jackson Lee was born in 1957 in Atlanta, Georgia. Lee's mother, Jacquelyn Shelton Lee taught arts and Black literature, and his father, William James Edward Lee III, was a professional jazz musician. Lee is the oldest of four children, and his siblings, Joie, David, and Cinqué, have all worked on his films. Jacquelyn began calling her son "Spike" because he had a prickly personality at a young age and was not afraid to voice his frank opinions. Lee later said his parents encouraged him to think for himself. He was taught to question the accuracy of what he read in the newspapers and saw on television news shows. Lee's parents also exposed him to the arts. His father played records and practiced jazz at home, and his mother took him to see Broadway plays and musicals. Lee also developed a love for sports, attending New York Mets baseball games and Knicks basketball games. Like most Black American children, Lee also had to deal with racism. He was not allowed to join the all-White Boy Scout troop in his predominantly Italian American neighborhood.

In 1975 Lee attended Morehouse College in Atlanta, a school that placed special emphasis on teaching about Black culture and history. While at Morehouse, Lee wrote a screenplay for what

Black Directors in the 1970s

When Spike Lee was a teenager in Brooklyn in the 1970s, he saw films made by a small group of Black directors that were controversial for the way they portrayed urban life. These films included *Sweet Sweetback's Baadasssss Song* (1971), directed by Melvin Van Peebles; *Shaft* (1971), directed by Gordon Parks; and *Superfly* (1972), directed by Gordon Parks Jr. The movies, later classified in a genre known as *blaxploitation* ("Black exploitation"), focused on the lives of pimps, prostitutes, drug dealers, and others struggling to survive in America's most neglected neighborhoods. Some viewers, including members of the civil rights organization the National Association for the Advancement of Colored People, spoke out against the negative Black stereotypes in these films. However, others celebrated the action-packed films for shining a light on social issues largely ignored by Hollywood. And Black characters in these films always managed to outsmart racist cops and other bullies. As Todd Boyd, a professor at the University of Southern California School of Cinematic Arts, explains, "This was really empowering to audiences because you had a black character who not only got the opportunity to tell off 'the man' and speak truth to power, but he did it with style. It was cool and had a flash to it. It's what people would now call 'woke.'"

Quoted in Tre'vell Anderson, "A Look Back at the Blaxploitation Era Through 2018 Eyes," *Los Angeles Times,* June 8, 2018. www.latimes.com.

would become his second film, *School Daze.* This work inspired him to become a filmmaker. But those who knew Lee doubted that this was a realistic career goal. One of Lee's professors, Herb Eichenberger, said, "You could only think of a few people who were black filmmakers . . . Gordon Parks, Melvin Van Peebles. And such people were not really recognized [by the film industry]. . . . [But Spike said] 'Hey, I want to make some changes.'"[27]

In order to make some changes, Lee majored in mass communications, which included classes in film, television production, radio, and print journalism. Lee made his first student film, *Last*

Hustle in Brooklyn, in 1977. The film documented what are called slice-of-life scenes on the streets of New York. The spontaneous shots included random people dancing the hustle in clubs and the chaos and looting that occurred during a citywide electricity blackout. After graduating from Morehouse, Lee moved back home to attend New York University's Tisch School of the Arts, where he earned a master of fine arts degree in film and television.

A New Direction for Black Cinema

Lee began working on his first feature-length film, *She's Gotta Have It,* in 1985 using a system that he continued to use for years. He woke up every morning at dawn and worked for three hours, writing down ideas by hand on yellow legal pads. Next, the best scenes were written on small index cards, which could be arranged into an order that best worked for the film. Lee then wrote out the script on notebook paper in longhand and put it together in a three-ring binder.

Director Spike Lee, seen here on the set of one of his movies, was among the first film makers to feature Black actors and actresses in all or most of a movie's lead roles. His widely popular films, including Do the Right Thing *(1989),* Malcolm X *(1992), and* BlacKkKlansman *(2018), strongly illuminated the state of race relations in the United States.*

She's Gotta Have It was one of the few films of that era to feature a Black female lead. Lee shot the film on a tight budget of $175,000, which he scraped together from grants, loans, and friends and family members willing to invest. As Lee recalled, "We had to put the money together nickel by nickel. It was the hardest thing I ever had to do."[28] Lee made the movie with unknown actors in the Fort Greene neighborhood of Brooklyn, and many of the cast and crew worked for free, hoping to be paid after the film was released.

Those who invested time or money in She's Gotta Have It were rewarded. Audiences and critics loved the film, which grossed more than $7.1 million in the United States alone. Film reviewer D.J.R. Bruckner explained why the movie was so different: "[She's Gotta Have It is] a groundbreaking film for African-American filmmakers and a welcome change in the representation of blacks in American cinema, depicting men and women of color not as pimps and whores, but as intelligent, upscale urbanites."[29] She's Gotta Have It went on to win two Independent Spirit Awards and awards from the Los Angeles Film Critics Association and the respected Cannes Film Festival in France.

> "[She's Gotta Have It is a] welcome change in the representation of blacks in American cinema, depicting men and women of color ... as intelligent, upscale urbanites."[29]
>
> —D.J.R. Bruckner, film reviewer

She's Gotta Have It was the first film produced by Lee's Brooklyn-based production company, 40 Acres and a Mule Filmworks. The name refers to a phrase that came into use just before the Civil War ended in 1865. Union general William Sherman promised liberated slaves in Georgia a land grant of 40 acres (16 ha) and a free army surplus mule. Lee's ironic use of the title is a reminder that the promise was never fulfilled.

Doing the Right Thing?

Although She's Gotta Have It did not generate much controversy, Do the Right Thing started a national conversation that resonated for years. In the final scene, a character named Mookie, played by Lee, is dismayed after the police kill his friend Radio Raheem. Mookie picks up a garbage can and throws it through the window of the pizzeria, inciting a riot. This left viewers to wonder whether Mookie—referring to the film's title—did the right thing. Some White film reviewers thought Mookie did the wrong thing. Writers at *New York* magazine, *Time,* and *USA Today* all claimed *Do the Right Thing* might incite Black moviegoers to start riots after they saw the film. In a 2014 interview on the twenty-fifth anniversary of the film's release, Lee was still bothered by these comments. "When I think about it, I just get mad. Because that was just outrageous, egregious and, I think, racist," he said. "I don't remember people saying people were going to come out of theatres killing people after they watched Arnold Schwarzenegger [action] films."[30] The critical reviews had little influence on audiences. The film, which cost $6 million to make, grossed over $37 million and won numerous awards.

The soundtrack for *Do the Right Thing* was composed and partially performed by Lee's father. The film also featured "Fight the Power," a hip-hop song by Public Enemy that was composed by the group at Lee's request. Lee produced and directed the video for the song. He would go on to produce more than a dozen videos for superstars such as Michael Jackson, Prince, and Eminem.

When Lee was a film student, he once told a friend that he would make one movie a year and achieve great success. Lee lived up to that dream after *Do the Right Thing*. His following films, *Mo' Better Blues* (1990) and *Jungle Fever* (1991) brought in millions of dollars and cemented Lee's reputation as the nation's hottest independent movie director.

Connecting Old Struggles to New

In 1992 Lee released one of his most ambitious films, *Malcolm X,* starring award-winning actor Denzel Washington. The epic biography, which ran for nearly three and a half hours, focused on the iconic civil rights activist who was assassinated in 1965. The film covered Malcolm X's life from the time the Ku Klux Klan terrorized his family when he was a child to his role as an outspoken advo-

Spike Lee's production company, 40 Acres and a Mule Filmworks, produced all his films beginning with *She's Gotta Have It* in 1986, along with music videos and commercials. 40 Acres and a Mule has also launched the careers of dozens of film professionals, including directors, producers, screenwriters, editors, cinematographers, actors, costume designers, and others who work behind the scenes to make movies. In 2004 Lee explained the objectives of the production company:

> From the very start, one of the goals at 40 Acres and a Mule was to demystify the whole filmmaking process. We wanted filmmaking to be accessible. It is a craft that can, and with serious study, be learned like anything else. We wanted people of color (male and female) to pursue careers in film, not only in front of the camera but, even more important, behind it. . . . [The roster] of all who got their start under the 40 Acres banner . . . is perhaps one of the greatest accomplishments of the 40 Acres and a Mule legacy.

Quoted in Kaleem Aftab, *Spike Lee: That's My Story and I'm Sticking to It*. New York: W.W. Norton, 2005, p. 305.

cate for Black Americans and a leader of the Nation of Islam. The epic biography of a complicated man and hero to millions was one of Lee's most critically acclaimed films.

The beginning of *Malcolm X* immediately grabbed the viewer's attention. Lee composed a shocking film montage of images that included an American flag burning into the shape of an *X* along with grainy footage of the 1991 beating of a Black motorist named Rodney King by five Los Angeles police officers. A voice-over of Washington as Malcolm delivers a fiery speech condemning the racism and brutality that Black Americans have faced for centuries. This film technique allowed Lee to connect Malcolm's activism in the 1960s to King's beating more than twenty-five years later.

In later years, Lee used this technique in several movies. His 2002 movie *25th Hour,* tells the story of a man during his last day of freedom as he prepares to go to prison for seven years. The film was being made when terrorists flew jet airplanes into the World Trade Center in New York on September 11, 2001, killing nearly three thousand people. Lee used some of the footage from the tragedy in *25th Hour.* As director Jordan Peele explains, "Spike pivoted and expertly wove the tragedy that befell his (and my) beloved city into his otherwise unrelated movie. But in the time since, no one has captured the spirit and heartbreak of post-9/11 New York as well as he did in the moment."[31]

In 2018 Lee once again mixed old and new images for *BlacKkKlansman.* The film was based on a true story about a Black police officer named Ron Stallworth who infiltrated the Ku Klux Klan in Colorado. *BlacKkKlansman* ends with a visual collage of the 2018 Unite the Right rally in Charlottesville, Virginia, where counterprotester Heather Heyer was run over and killed by a neo-Nazi. According to Peele, the scene "was a reminder that even though the Ron Stallworth story was decades old, the hatred he fought was still very fresh. It was also a testament to Spike's ability as a filmmaker to transcend history."[32]

While transcending history, Lee surpassed the traditional role of filmmakers. Whether he is making a horror movie, a comedy, a drama, or a biography based on true events, Lee dependably mixes compelling imagery with provocative calls to action. And in his public statements, Lee never fails to point out the violence and discrimination people of color have faced throughout American history. But as writer and producer Cheo Hodari Coker points out, "People talk about Spike's politics all the time but they never talk about his skills. He is the most visually accomplished director out there. Period. Nobody shoots like Spike."[33] And Lee's writing, directing, and producing skills continue to inspire young filmmakers to make movies that are fresh, relevant, and stunning to watch.

CHAPTER FOUR

Tupac Shakur: Rapper

On September 13, 1996, hip-hop superstar Tupac Amaru Shakur, known as 2Pac, died after being targeted in a drive-by shooting in Las Vegas. Shakur's mother, Afeni Shakur, described his last minutes: "The doctor came out and said that Tupac had stopped breathing. Three times. And they revived him three times. And that every time they revived him, he just went back. And I asked them to leave him alone and let him go. . . . I really felt it was important for Tupac, who fought so hard to have a free spirit. I thought it was important for his spirit to be allowed to be free."[34]

Millions mourned Shakur's death at the age of twenty-five in a crime that remains unsolved. Shakur touched listeners' souls and inspired countless rappers with his gangsta rap that focused on racism, crime, police shootings, gangs, and drugs. Shakur's rhymes made him one of the best-selling artists of all time. As of 2020, he had sold more than 75 million albums worldwide.

A Young Revolutionary

Tupac was born Lesane Parish Crooks in 1971 in the Harlem neighborhood of New York City. Tupac's father, Billy Garland, was not part of his life. Afeni renamed her son when he was one year old. She wanted him to bear the name of Túpac Amaru II, whose name translates as "shining serpent." Amaru was an Incan ruler in Peru

The terms *hip-hop* and *rap* are used interchangeably to describe the musical style that exploded in popularity in the late 1980s. The growth of hip-hop was driven by gangsta rap. This style of music featured aggressive rhymes about urban life in American cities where millions of young Black people were unemployed and neighborhoods were flooded with a highly addictive type of cocaine called crack. Amid this grim situation, the Los Angeles rap group N.W.A. released its debut album *Straight Outta Compton* in 1988.

The raw anger, aggression, obscenity, homophobia, and antipolice raps on the record shocked authorities and ignited a firestorm in the media. But *Straight Outta Compton* marked the beginning of the gangsta rap era, when a new generation of rap acts such as Tupac Shakur and the Notorious B.I.G. (Christopher George Latore Wallace) wrote songs focused on gangs, violence, sex, cannabis, crack, materialism, fighting the police, and the brutality of inner-city life. Although gangsta rappers sold millions of albums, sales were not driven by inner-city youths. Eighty percent of those who purchased *Straight Outta Compton* were White suburban teens. These sales made gangsta rap the most lucrative form of hip-hop during the 1990s.

who was executed in 1791 after leading a failed revolt against Spanish conquerors.

Afeni was considered a revolutionary herself by the government. She was a leader in the New York division of the Black Panther Party, a national political group founded in 1966 to protest police brutality and Black poverty. In 1969 Afeni was arrested and charged with conspiracy and attempted murder in a Black Panther plot to bomb police stations and banks. After spending eight months in prison, pregnant with Tupac, she was found not guilty of the charges against her. Afeni was released one month before Tupac was born and soon left the Black Panther Party. But she continued to work as an activist who wanted to change the world, a message she instilled in her son. When Tupac was ten years old, a preacher at the House of the Lord Church in Brooklyn asked him what he wanted to be when he grew up. He boldly said, "I want to be a revolutionary."[35]

As a child, Shakur channeled his revolutionary instincts into artistic and creative endeavors. At age twelve he attended a Harlem theater group called the 127th Street Ensemble. Shakur acted in the play *A Raisin in the Sun*, which tells the story of a Black family moving to an all-White Chicago suburb to escape poverty. Shakur enjoyed acting and viewed it as a way to escape the hardships in his own life of poverty.

Acting, Dancing, and Rapping

Shakur was already writing poems at age thirteen, when he moved to Baltimore with his mother and his eleven-year-old half sister, Sekyiwa. Two years later, Shakur was accepted as a theater student at the Baltimore School for the Arts (BSA). Donald Hicken, head of the school's theater department, saw a special spark when Shakur auditioned for the school as the character he had played in *A Raisin in the Sun*: "The empathy, the [actor's] instinct, the emotional connection, the vulnerability. He had all of that."[36] In addition to acting, Shakur studied poetry, jazz, and even ballet dancing. He was especially fond of the works of William Shakespeare; Shakur believed Shakespeare's plays, such as *King Lear* and *Hamlet,* reflected the drama and violence of gang warfare in the 1980s. As Shakur said in 1995, "[Shakespeare] wrote the rawest stories, man."[37]

Shakur wrote his own raw stories. By 1987 Afeni was addicted to crack cocaine, which left her family in dire poverty. "Yeah, we didn't have any lights at home in my house. No lights, no electricity," Shakur later recalled. "And [the hip-hop song] 'I'm Bad' by L.L. Cool J came out and I had batteries in my radio. I heard it for the first time and I was writing rhymes by candlelight and I knew I was gonna be a rapper."[38] Shakur was already very popular at school, and students were further drawn to him when he started rapping. Classmate Becky Mossing later recalled, "He just had a magnetism that defied logic, and everybody was drawn to him. Everyone wanted to hear what he had to say."[39]

Connecting in California

Students could hear Shakur expressing himself in rap battles he held with his friend and BSA schoolmate Jada Pinkett, a young singer, songwriter, and actor. Shakur wrote poems about Pinkett, who went on to launch a show business career and marry movie star Will Smith.

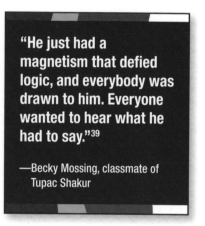

"He just had a magnetism that defied logic, and everybody was drawn to him. Everyone wanted to hear what he had to say."[39]

—Becky Mossing, classmate of Tupac Shakur

Shakur never got to graduate from BSA. In 1988 Afeni moved the family to Marin City, California, hoping to escape Baltimore's drug culture. At the time, this small community north of San Francisco was mired in poverty, drugs, and violence. Shakur hated leaving BSA and later said his life got off track when he had to leave the arts high school. In Marin City, he fought with his mother, sold drugs, slept on friends' couches, and scrounged constantly for meals.

Despite his situation Shakur kept dreaming of stardom. He joined a six-member rap group, Strictly Dope, which performed at local clubs. Strictly Dope did not last long. But through the group, Shakur met a hip-hop concert promoter named Leila Steinberg, who became his first manager. Steinberg helped Shakur get into a popular rap group called Digital Underground. In early 1991 Shakur adopted the stage name "2Pac" and rapped on the Digital Underground single "Same Song." Shakur appeared in the music video of "Same Song," and the single was used in the soundtrack for the Dan Ackroyd movie *Nothing but Trouble.* Shakur appeared briefly in the film, which was a box-office bomb.

Digital Underground exposed Shakur to life in a professional hip-hop group. He spent hours in the recording studio watching group members sample sounds, create beats, and record raps. Digital Underground also went on numerous tours, performing throughout the United States, Japan, and Europe. Being in a group gave Shakur the opportunity to record his own demo, which was produced by Digital Underground front man Shock G (Gregory Jacobs).

2Pacalypse Now

Shakur's demo made its way to the desk of Ted Field, who cofounded Interscope Records with famed record producer Jimmy Iovine. Field gave the demo to his teenage daughter, who was impressed by Shakur's music and his movie star good looks. In November

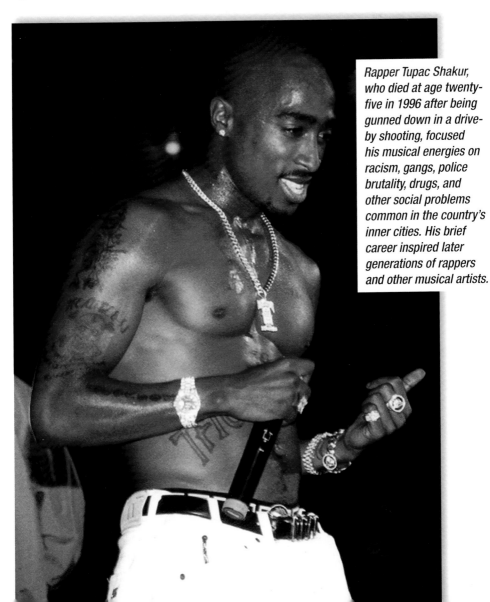

Rapper Tupac Shakur, who died at age twenty-five in 1996 after being gunned down in a drive-by shooting, focused his musical energies on racism, gangs, police brutality, drugs, and other social problems common in the country's inner cities. His brief career inspired later generations of rappers and other musical artists.

1991 Interscope released Shakur's debut album, *2Pacalypse Now*. Not long after *2Pacalypse Now* was released, Shakur explained the concepts on the album: "It's all about addressing the problems that we face in everyday society. Police brutality, poverty, unemployment, insufficient education, disunity, violence, black-on-black crime, teenage pregnancy, and crack addiction."[40]

Shakur did not hold back on his seething anger when he rapped about the injustices he saw all around him. In "Trapped," Shakur compares poverty-stricken urban neighborhoods to prisons where escape is impossible. The song "Brenda's Got a Baby" was based on the true story of a twelve-year-old impregnated by a family member and who later abandoned her baby. Brenda becomes a prostitute before she is senselessly murdered. Shakur said the track was the only rap song that addressed problems faced by young girls. "It talked about child molestation. . . . It talked about the effects of poverty," he said. "It talked about how one person's problems can affect a whole community of people. It talked about how the innocent are the ones that get hurt."[41]

Thug Life

When *2Pacalypse Now* was first released, it was not a blockbuster album—it peaked at number sixty-four on the Billboard 200 album charts and number thirteen on the Top R&B/Hip-Hop Albums chart. But the album grabbed the media's attention while angering some of the most powerful politicians in the country. In the song "Soulja's Story," Shakur tells the tale of an alienated young Black man who shoots a police officer. Five months after the song was released, a young Black man allegedly listening to the song while driving a stolen truck shot and killed a Texas state trooper. Later that year, Vice President Dan Quayle tried to get Interscope to pull the record from stores, saying, "There's no reason for a record like this to be released. It has no place in our society."[42] The Texas officer's family later attempted, unsuccessfully, to sue Shakur. Ironically, the publicity added to the album's popularity, pumped up sales, and made Shakur a superstar.

The controversy prevented Shakur from booking concerts in some areas because promoters were afraid that his violent rap lyrics might start riots. But Shakur was surprised that his work had become the focus of politicians and other national critics. As Shakur told journalist Chuck Philips in 1993,

> I started out saying I was down for the young black male, you know, and that was gonna be my thang. I just wanted to rap about things that affected young black males. When I said that, I didn't know that I was gonna tie myself down to just take all the blunts and hits for all the young black males, to be the media's kicking post for young black males. I just figured since I lived that life I could do that, I could rap about that.[43]

Tupac Against the World

Shakur had a large tattoo across his midriff that read "Thug Life," and he remained a divisive figure, with controversy following him into his personal life. In 1993 he was accused of sexual assault, a charge he strongly denied. In November 1994 Shakur was shot five times in a robbery in his New York studio. Shakur survived but the crime remained unsolved. The day after the shooting the bandaged Shakur, sitting in a wheelchair, was sentenced to nine months in prison on the sexual assault charge. He began serving time after his recovery.

While he was in prison in early 1995, Shakur's previously recorded album *Me Against the World* was released. The rapper's notoriety helped boost his fame, and the album sold 240,000 copies in the first week. *Me Against the World* hit number one on the Billboard 200 chart and stayed there for four weeks. *Me Against the World* set

> "I just wanted to rap about things that affected young black males. When I said that, I didn't know that I was gonna . . . be the media's kicking post for young black males."[43]
>
> —Tupac Shakur

Tupac's Big Mouth

In a 1994 MTV interview, Tupac Shakur was asked what he thought he would be remembered for. Shakur's answer revealed his insight into his own strengths and shortcomings:

> My big mouth. I got a big mouth. I can't help it, I talk from my heart, I'm real. You know what I'm sayin'? Whatever comes, comes. But it's not my fault. I'm trying to find my way in the world. I'm trying to be somebody instead of making money off everybody. . . . So I go down paths that haven't been traveled before. And I usually mess up, but I learn. I come back stronger. I'm not talkin' about ignorant. So obviously I put thought into what I do. So I think [what I'll be remembered for is] my mouth and my controversy. I haven't been out of the paper since I joined Digital Underground. And that's good for me cuz I don't want to be forgotten. If I'm forgotten then that means I'm comfortable and that means I think everything is OK.

Quoted in Armond White, *Rebel for the Hell of It*. New York: Thunder Mouth, 2002, p. 175.

two records: Shakur was the first male solo hip-hop artist to sell that many records in one week, and he was the first artist of any genre to have a number one record while in prison.

When Shakur released the two-volume album *All Eyez on Me* in February 1996, it sold 5 million copies within two months and produced two number-one singles: "How Do U Want It" and "California Love." *All Eyez on Me* was to be Shakur's last record. Eight months after the album was released, Shakur was shot and killed in Las Vegas. Although it was never proved, many in the hip-hop community believed the rapper the Notorious B.I.G. (known as "Biggie") was behind the murder. Six months later, Biggie was killed by an unknown assailant in a drive-by shooting in Los Angeles.

In 2017, more than two decades after his death, Shakur became the first solo rapper to be inducted into the Rock and Roll Hall of Fame. Hip-hop superstar Snoop Dogg explained Shakur's influence during the induction speech:

> While many remember him now as some kind of thugged-out superhero, Tupac knew he was only human, and he represented through his music like no one before. . . . With an unapologetic rawness, 'Pac embraced those contradictions that proved we ain't just a character out of someone else's storybook. To be human is to be many things at once; strong and vulnerable; hard-headed and intellectual; courageous and afraid; loving, and vengeful; revolutionary and—oh yeah . . . gangsta.[44]

Changing the Culture

In 2020 hip-hop record sales surpassed those of rock and roll, and songs by rappers made up nearly one-third of all music streams in the United States. The music style also dominated YouTube: the top ten most-viewed artists were rappers, including Young-Boy, Lil Baby, and Drake. These hip-hop artists, and thousands of others, owe a debt of gratitude to Tupac Shakur. He turned a bright light on issues that mainstream culture preferred to ignore.

Shakur was a skilled poet and storyteller with a powerful voice. In the studio, he was a master of sampling, vocal layering, and other recording techniques used to create the memorable beats that backed up his words. While making his dream of rap stardom come true, Shakur changed the language, transformed fashion, and forever altered the sound of popular music.

CHAPTER FIVE

Misty Copeland: Ballet Dancer

In 2015 Misty Copeland seemed to be everywhere. Copeland, thirty-two, could be seen dancing ballet on New York City stages. She was named to the *Time* magazine 100 Most Influential People list that year and was profiled on the television news show *60 Minutes.* And Copeland blew up on social media after an ad she made for Under Armour was viewed more than 8 million times. This amount of attention would be unusual for any ballet dancer. But Copeland was not just any ballet dancer. She was the first Black woman to be named principal dancer in the seventy-five-year history of the prestigious American Ballet Theatre (ABT). The principal dancer is the highest rank in a dance company, and those who serve in this role are the best of the best. Journalist Chloe Angyal later made the distinction clear: "In America . . . there are two classes of professional ballet dancers: There's Misty Copeland, and then there's everyone else."[45]

Those who witness Copeland leaping through the air in front of sold-out crowds might forget that she grew up extremely poor. Copeland was born in 1982 in St. Louis. Her family moved to Southern California when she was very young. Copeland's mother, Sylvia DelaCerna, studied dance and was once a cheerleader for the Kansas City Chiefs football team. Doug Copeland, father to Misty and her three older siblings, was not part of the family.

Misty also had two younger half siblings from her mother's third and fourth marriages.

Spinning and Dancing

In 1989 Copeland found a role model after watching the television movie *Nadia* about the young Romanian gymnast Nadia Comăneci. In 1976, fourteen-year-old Comăneci became the first female to achieve a perfect score of 10 in Olympic gymnastics. She took home three gold medals and won two more in the 1980 Olympics. Copeland taped *Nadia* and watched it over and over, imitating the gymnast, perfecting cartwheels, splits, and other moves. As Copeland wrote in her memoir, *Life in Motion: An Unlikely Ballerina*, "I would pretend to be Nadia after I finished my routines, raising my arms with pride for the imaginary crowd."[46] Pop star Mariah Carey was another role model. Copeland choreographed dance moves to perform with Carey's music videos.

Copeland had another role model. Her older sister Erica had been the captain of the Dana Middle School dance team in San Pedro, California. When it was Copeland's time to attend the school, she auditioned for the dance team and was made its new captain. The dance team's coach, Elizabeth Cantine, was a classically trained ballet dancer who was impressed by Copeland's fluid movements, poise, and athleticism.

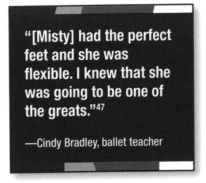

"[Misty] had the perfect feet and she was flexible. I knew that she was going to be one of the greats."[47]

—Cindy Bradley, ballet teacher

In early 1995 Cantine recommended that Copeland attend free weekly ballet classes taught by her friend Cindy Bradley at the Boys & Girls Club of San Pedro. Copeland knew nothing about ballet, but Bradley saw something magical in the way she moved. "I've never been able to put it in to words exactly, the feeling that I got. But it was almost like a vision of what she could be one day," Bradley recalled in 2015. "She had the perfect feet and she was flexible. I knew that she was going to be one of the greats."[47]

Being a great ballet dancer was the last thing on Copeland's mind. At the time, she was living with her mother and five siblings in two small rooms at a cheap motel. In addition to her family's lack of funds, Copeland had another strike against her: most professional ballet dancers take their first lessons when they are five years old or younger. At age thirteen, Copeland was considered very old for a beginner. But she had the ability to expertly mimic any ballet steps she saw. Although it takes many young ballerinas up to three years to dance gracefully on their toes (a position called *en point*), Copeland mastered it in three months.

Family Conflict

Copeland said once she started ballet lessons, she was excited to dance every day. She started dedicating all her spare time to practicing at Bradley's studio, the San Pedro Dance Center. Some nights Copeland would not return to the motel until after dark. This created a conflict between Bradley and Copeland's mother. DelaCerna thought the ballet lessons were taking up too much of Copeland's time. But Bradley convinced DelaCerna to let Copeland live with her near her dance studio.

"Technique is taught, but there are things that just can't be taught. And Misty is an artist. . . . She dances with real joy."[48]

—Barbara Haig, Los Angeles Music Center competition coordinator

After three years of lessons under Bradley's guidance, Copeland was an emerging star. And in the highly competitive world of ballet dancing, Copeland had few equals. In 1997 she won first place in the Los Angeles Music Center Spotlight Awards, open to all high school students in Southern California. Competition coordinator Barbara Haig even noted, "Technique is taught, but there are things that just can't be taught. And Misty is an artist. . . . She dances with real joy."[48]

Winners of Spotlight Awards often go on to join the world's most prestigious ballet companies, such as the ABT and the Joffrey Ballet. But DelaCerna felt like she was losing her daughter and

A Grueling Practice Schedule

Every year the American Ballet Theatre gives performances during a month-long fall season and a two-month-long spring season. Dancers also perform Tchaikovsky's famous ballet *The Nutcracker* for about one month during the winter holiday season. Ballet dancers in these shows maintain a grueling practice schedule, as Copeland explains in her autobiography, *Life in Motion: An Unlikely Ballerina*:

> We train very hard during the year. When we're still working on ballets for our seasonal shows, we dance for about nine hours a day. Our morning begins with a ballet class that lasts an hour and a half. We practice our barre and center work so that we can keep up our strength and technique. Then we work on the ballets we'll be performing for seven hours, from noon until seven o'clock at night. Once we've started performing, we dance even longer. Our evenings end just before midnight. . . . Our bodies are our instruments, and ballet is so demanding that it's essential for dancers to stay in shape. I also keep my body toned through other classes, like cardio and a series of exercises called Pilates. It's important to maintain our technique and physical fitness because that's how we're chosen for roles in different ballets.

Misty Copeland, *Life in Motion: An Unlikely Ballerina*. New York: Aladdin, 2016, pp. 81–82.

ordered her to move back in with her family. Copeland later recalled, "I did not want to lose ballet. And the thought of losing that and coming back and living at this motel was something that I just couldn't let happen. It was like watching my future slip away."[49]

At the age of fifteen, Copeland turned to the courts. She filed what are called emancipation papers, which are legal documents that would allow Copeland to be lawfully considered an adult for most business matters. The proceedings turned into a bitter legal feud between DelaCerna and Bradley, with Copeland in the middle. As Copeland's attorney, Steve Bartell, explains, "[Misty] was caught between a rock and a hard place. . . . She was afraid that if she went back to her mother, she'd never dance again."[50] The fight became a public matter after it made headlines in the *Los Angeles Times*, and local television news cameras began covering the court proceedings. Copeland finally relented. She dropped her bid for independence and moved back in with her mother. But she did not stop dancing.

Misty Copeland, seen here performing on stage, became the first Black woman to be hired as principal dancer in the entire seventy-five-year history of the American Ballet Theatre, among the top ballet companies in the world. Highly versatile, she has appeared in both classical pieces, like Swan Lake, *and contemporary ones, such as* West Side Story.

Intensive Training

In 1998 Copeland won a scholarship for gifted young dancers at the ABT summer program in New York City. Copeland's co-ordination and instinctive physical response to music attracted the attention of theater director Kevin McKenzie. He believed she had all the elements to become a major ballet star. But as Copeland writes, working toward this goal was incredibly difficult, even for someone with her natural talent: "The summer intensive was fun but exhausting. We spent seven hours a day practicing our technique. Then we'd go home with swollen feet and tired muscles."[51]

Copeland returned to the ABT Summer Intensive Program on full scholarship for two more years. During this period, Copeland worked with esteemed choreographer Twyla Tharp. In 2000, Copeland was asked to join the ABT studio company, where promising young ballet dancers train before moving to the theater's main company.

Copeland was promoted to the ABT's main company in 2001. She appeared in Tchaikovsky's ballet *The Sleeping Beauty* and was chosen to play the lead role in *The Nutcracker.* But a sharp pain in her lower back forced Copeland to revise her plans. Tests revealed that she had a lumbar stress fracture, an injury common to ballet dancers caused by repeatedly bending backward. Copeland spent the next six months in a back brace that she could only remove while bathing. After another six months in physical therapy, Copeland was ready to dance. But the stress caused by long hours of practice often delays puberty in female ballet dancers. This was happening to Copeland; her bones were brittle, and her body was not growing like it was supposed to. A doctor put her on hormones, and she gained more than 10 pounds (4.5 kg) and, as Copeland put it, her body became curvy. Copeland was extremely self-conscious in her new body, thinking she was fat even though at 5 feet 2 inches (1.5 meters) tall she only weighed 108 pounds (49 kg).

Finding Mentors

Copeland had other doubts when she danced. There was one Black male dancer at the ABT, Danny Tidwell (who left in 2005), but she was the only woman of color in a ballet company of around eighty people. And most dancers, except for soloists, are supposed to move as one and look as similar as possible. As Copeland said in 2015, she had to push back against stereotypes. "[Black ballet dancers are] told they don't fit in, they won't have a successful career, they don't have the bodies," she recalled. "Even to this day I hear that I shouldn't even be wearing a tutu. I don't have the right legs. My muscles are too big."[52]

> [Black ballet dancers are] told they don't fit in, they won't have a successful career, they don't have the bodies. Even to this day I hear that I shouldn't even be wearing a tutu. I don't have the right legs. My muscles are too big."[52]
>
> —Misty Copeland, ballet dancer

Copeland had trouble finding anyone in the company who understood her situation, and she often felt isolated. However, she found a mentor in Susan Fales-Hill, a biracial writer and vice-chair of the ABT board of directors that oversees the ballet company. Fales-Hill became Copeland's sponsor, guiding her through the world of professional ballet while providing emotional support. Fales-Hill connected Copeland to a squad of Black female trailblazers to offer guidance. They included the pioneering Black actress Diahann Carroll, runway model and writer Veronica Webb, and Raven Wilkinson, a ballet dancer who, in 1955, became the first Black woman to dance with a major ballet company.

With the help of her mentors, Copeland regained her confidence as her career took off. She had a breakthrough year in 2004, gaining widespread recognition for her outstanding performances in *Raymonda, Pillar of Fire, Swan Lake,* and other ballets. Copeland also experienced a personal milestone that year: she met her father for the first time. It was such a positive experience, father and daughter have remained in close contact.

As the only Black woman in the American Ballet Theatre, Misty Copeland struggled with feelings of isolation and depression. She found a mentor in Raven Wilkinson, who became the first Black dancer in a major American ballet company in 1955. Wilkinson was born in 1935 in New York City and began studying ballet at age nine. When Wilkinson was twenty, she began performing in the Ballet Russe de Monte-Carlo, based in New York. Wilkinson, who was light-skinned, was told not to let the public know she was Black. She was required to wear white makeup on stage. When the company toured in the South, Wilkinson was barred from staying with the other dancers in segregated hotels where Black customers were not welcome.

Wilkinson, one of the greatest ballet dancers of the era, was exhausted by the racism she faced. She left the world of professional ballet in 1961 to teach and give lectures. In 1967 Wilkinson joined the Dutch National Ballet as a principal dancer. By the time she returned to the United States in 1974, the ballet color barriers had broken down. Wilkinson danced with the New York City Opera until 1985. She befriended Copeland in 2015 and died at age eighty-three in 2018.

Dancing with Prince

Copeland was twenty-five in 2007 when she became the youngest dancer to be promoted to soloist at the ABT. She was also the first Black soloist at the ABT in almost twenty years. Ballet companies have around twelve soloists who get leading solo roles to show off their abilities. Copeland calls soloists the cream of the crop, and press reviews referred to her as a rising star. During her first year as a soloist, Copeland danced in several ballets considered avant-garde or modern because they were composed after 1940. These ballets allowed Copeland to improvise movements in ways she could not when performing traditional ballets. One

51

review for Twyla Tharp's *Baker's Dozen* noted, "Copeland who brought a jolt of electricity to [*Baker's Dozen*] has always been a compelling dancer. But here she was sensuous, dramatic, and sophisticated in an entirely new, contemporary way."[53]

Copeland's positive reviews attracted the attention of a ballet-loving superstar. In 2009 a friend texted Copeland to say Prince wanted her phone number. Copeland responded, "Prince who, prince of what? What are you talking about?"[54] Her friend was referring to the legendary funk rock musician Prince, who invited Copeland to Los Angeles to perform in a music video.

Prince's trippy remake of the 1968 song "Crimson and Clover" video features Copeland twirling, leaping, and elongating her body in a breathtaking dance she choreographed. The two remained friends, and in 2011 Copeland accompanied Prince as a guest artist on his United States concert tour. Copeland later described the experience: "I felt at the top of my game when I was collaborating with Prince. His faith in me made me feel like I was finally a professional. I felt like I was in charge of my career, being celebrated for what I do best by such a successful artist. I felt like a true ballerina."[55]

Copeland's performances with Prince also raised her profile with a mainstream audience that was not familiar with ballet. Copeland said young Black girls began stopping her on the street or in the subway saying they wanted to become ballet dancers. She told them to do it, there was no reason they could not pursue their dreams. "Hopefully I can set that example so they don't give up,"[56] she said.

A Principal Dancer

Copeland's example could be seen on ballet stages throughout the world. She danced in leading roles in major ballets and created new dances for *The Nutcracker* and *The Sleeping Beauty.* And she became a role model for kids of all backgrounds and levels of talent when she was named the National Youth of the Year Ambassador for the Boys & Girls Clubs of America in 2013. Copeland was thirty-three years old in 2015 when she was appointed principal ballerina at the ABT. Although Black ballerinas have been principals at smaller companies, Copeland was the first at a major international company.

Principal ballerinas need to be more than technically perfect. They are required to communicate complex emotions and ideas with their movements and use acting skills to play characters in story ballets such as *The Nutcracker.* Copeland used her talents to take on other roles. As reviewer Gia Kourlas noted, Copeland "lit up the stage"[57] when she acted, danced, and even sang in the Broadway play *On the Town.* Copeland did some voice acting, playing herself in the animated 2016 television series *Peg + Cat.* And she modeled for *Harper's Bazaar* and other publications.

Copeland released two books in 2014: her memoir, *Life in Motion*, and *Firebird*, a picture book with a story meant to empower young girls of color. Her health and fitness guide, *Ballerina Body,* was published in 2017. Although Copeland tries to keep her fame in perspective, she is easily the most famous ballerina in the world. And she is proud of her achievements, as she writes in the opening lines of *Life in Motion:*

> I think that people think that I sometimes focus too much on the fact that I'm a black dancer. But there's never been a black principal woman at the Royal Ballet. At the Paris Opera Ballet. At the Kirov Ballet, in the top companies in the world. In New York City Ballet, in New York City. I don't think that people realize what a feat it is being a black woman. But that's so much of who I am, and I think it's so much a part of my story.[58]

SOURCE NOTES

Introduction: The Black Roots of American Culture

1. Quoted in George E. Mowry, *The Twenties: Fords, Flappers & Fanatics*. Englewood Cliffs, NJ: Prentice-Hall, 1963, p. 66.
2. Quoted in Paul Sorene, "Cab Calloway's Hepster's Dictionary: A Guide to the Language of Jive (1938)," Flashbak, April 26, 2017. https://flashbak.com.
3. Quoted in David Zurawik, "PBS Treats Baltimore's Cab Calloway as an American Master," *Baltimore Sun,* February 27, 2012. www.baltimoresun.com.

Chapter One
Maya Angelou: Writer and Activist

4. Quoted in Sangeeta Singh-Kurtz, "Beyoncé's Documentary Trailer Presents Her as the Best the Human Race Has to Offer," Quartz, April 8, 2019. https://qz.com.
5. Rachel Nuwer, "Maya Angelou Was One of the Most Influential Voices of Our Time," *Smithsonian Magazine,* May 28, 2014. www.smithsonianmag.com.
6. Maya Angelou, *I Know Why the Caged Bird Sings.* New York: Random House, 2009, p. 87.
7. Quoted in Lucinda Moore, "Growing Up Maya Angelou," *Smithsonian Magazine,* April 2003. www.smithsonianmag.com.
8. Quoted in Moore, "Growing Up Maya Angelou."
9. Maya Angelou, *The Heart of a Woman.* New York: Random House, 1981, p. 106.
10. Quoted in Dinitia Smith, "A Career in Letters, 50 Years and Counting," *New York Times,* January 23, 2007. www.nytimes.com.
11. Oprah Winfrey, foreword to *I Know Why the Caged Bird Sings*, by Maya Angelou. New York: Random House, 2009, p. 6.
12. Quoted in Meredith Berkman, "Media Star Maya Angelou," *Entertainment Weekly*, February 26, 1993. https://ew.com.

13. Quoted in Moore, "Growing Up Maya Angelou."

Chapter Two
Aretha Franklin: Soul Singer

14. Quoted in Anna North, "The Political and Cultural Impact of Aretha Franklin's 'Respect,' Explained," *Vox*, August 17, 2018. www.vox .com.
15. Rob Sheffield, "Why Aretha Franklin Was America's Greatest Voice," *Rolling Stone*, August 17, 2018. www.rollingstone.com.
16. Quoted in Mark Bego, *Aretha Franklin: The Queen of Soul*. New York: Skyhorse, 2012, p. 17.
17. Quoted in David Ritz, *Respect: The Life of Aretha Franklin*. New York: Little, Brown, 2014, p. 32.
18. Quoted in Ritz, *Respect*, pp. 64–65.
19. Quoted in Bego, *Aretha Franklin*, p. 83.
20. Quoted in Ritz, *Respect*, p. 493.
21. Sheffield, "Why Aretha Franklin Was America's Greatest Voice."
22. Quoted in Bego, *Aretha Franklin*, p. 17.
23. Quoted in North, "The Political and Cultural Impact of Aretha Franklin's 'Respect,' Explained."

Chapter Three
Spike Lee: Filmmaker

24. Quoted in Uday Bhatia, "Radio Raheem's Death in Spike Lee's 'Do the Right Thing' Still Haunts America," *Mint*, June 3, 2020. www .livemint.com.
25. Quoted in Andre M. Perry and Tawanna Black, "George Floyd's Death Demonstrates the Policy Violence That Devalues Black Lives," *The Avenue* (blog), Brookings Institution, May 28, 2020. www.brookings.edu.
26. Quoted in Bhatia, "Radio Raheem's Death in Spike Lee's 'Do the Right Thing' Still Haunts America."
27. Quoted in Kaleem Aftab, *Spike Lee: That's My Story and I'm Sticking to It*. New York: W.W. Norton, 2005, pp. 11–12.
28. Quoted in Aftab, *Spike Lee*, p. 31.
29. D.J.R. Bruckner, "*She's Gotta Have It* (1986)," *New York Times*, August 9, 1986, Section C, p. 14. https://timesmachine.nytimes.com.
30. Quoted in Gavid Edwards, "Fight the Power: Spike Lee on 'Do the Right Thing,'" *Rolling Stone*, June 20, 2014. www.rollingstone.com.
31. Jordan Peele, "Spike Lee," *Time* 100, 2019. https://time.com.
32. Peele, "Spike Lee."

33. Quoted in Mekeisha Madden Toby, "With 'Do the Right Thing,' Spike Lee Changed Cinema Forever," *Shondaland*, June 26, 2019. www.shondaland.com.

Chapter Four
Tupac Shakur: Rapper

34. Quoted in Armond White, *Rebel for the Hell of It.* New York: Thunder Mouth, 2002, p. xv.
35. Quoted in White, *Rebel for the Hell of It,* p. 1.
36. Quoted in Wesley Case, "Tupac Shakur in Baltimore: Friends, Teachers Remember the Birth of an Artist," *Baltimore Sun,* March 11, 2017. www.baltimoresun.com.
37. Quoted in L-Fresh the Lion and Rosa Gollan, "Tupac Was One of the Greatest Rappers of All Time and Here's Why," ABC National Radio, September 5, 2017. www.abc.net.au.
38. Quoted in White, *Rebel for the Hell of It,* p. 13.
39. Quoted in Case, "Tupac Shakur in Baltimore."
40. Quoted in Justin Chadwick, "2Pac's Debut Album '2Pacalypse Now' Turns 25," Albumism, November 10, 2016. www.albumism.com.
41. Quoted in CR Fashion, "Why *2Pacalypse Now* Is More Important than Ever," June 16, 2020. www.crfashionbook.com.
42. Quoted in Chadwick, "2Pac's Debut Album '2Pacalypse Now' Turns 25."
43. Quoted in Sami Yenigun, "20 Years Ago, Tupac Broke Through," *Morning Edition,* NPR, July 19, 2013. www.npr.org.
44. Quoted in Peter A. Berry, "Read the Full Transcript of Snoop Dogg's 2Pac Speech at 2017 Rock and Roll Hall of Fame Induction Ceremony," *XXL,* April 8, 2017. www.xxlmag.com.

Chapter Five
Misty Copeland: Ballet Dancer

45. Chloe Angyal, "The Meaning of Misty Copeland," *Glamour,* March 8, 2021. www.glamour.com.
46. Misty Copeland, *Life in Motion: An Unlikely Ballerina.* New York: Aladdin, 2016, p. 12.
47. Quoted in Bill Whitaker, "Misty Copeland," *60 Minutes,* May 10, 2015. www.cbsnews.com.
48. Quoted in Deborah Hastings, "Teen Dancer Stumbles in Adults' Tug-of-War," South Coast Today, November 1, 1998. www.south coasttoday.com.
49. Quoted in Whitaker, "Misty Copeland."

50. Quoted in Hastings, "Teen Dancer Stumbles in Adults' Tug-of-War."
51. Copeland, *Life in Motion,* p. 70.
52. Quoted in Whitaker, "Misty Copeland."
53. Roslyn Sulcas, "Odes to an Ax Murderer from New England and a Singer from Hoboken," *New York Times,* November 6, 2007. www.nytimes.com.
54. Quoted in Astrida Woods, "Misty's Magic," *Dance,* November 10, 2010. www.dancemagazine.com.
55. Copeland, *Life in Motion*, pp. 135–36.
56. Quoted in Woods, "Misty's Magic."
57. Gia Kourlas, "Misty Copeland Makes Her Broadway Debut in 'On the Town," *New York Times,* August 26, 2015. www.nytimes.com.
58. Quoted in Leah Donnella, "Misty Copeland Achieves #SquadGoals in the Documentary 'A Ballerina's Tale,'" *Code Switch,* NPR, February 16, 2016. www.npr.org.

FOR FURTHER RESEARCH

Books (Nonfiction)

Misty Copeland, *Life in Motion: An Unlikely Ballerina*. New York: Aladdin, 2016.

Stuart Kallen, *Kendrick Lamar*. San Diego: ReferencePoint, 2020.

Bill O'Neill, *The Great Book of Black Heroes: 30 Fearless and Inspirational Black Men and Women That Changed History*. Sheridan, WY: LAK, 2021.

Tamara Pizzoli, *Bold Words from Black Women: Inspiration and Truths from 50 Extraordinary Leaders Who Helped Shape Our World*. New York: Denene Millner, 2022.

Books (Fiction and Poetry)

Maya Angelou, *I Know Why the Caged Bird Sings*. New York: Random House, 2009.

Tupac Shakur, *The Rose That Grew from Concrete*. London: Simon & Schuster, 2006.

Internet Sources

"50 Most Important African American Music Artists of All Time," Advance Local Media, 2021. www.cleveland.com.

Justin Chadwick, "2Pac's Debut Album '2Pacalypse Now' Turns 25," Albumism, November 10, 2016. www.albumism.com.

Lucinda Moore, "Growing Up Maya Angelou," *Smithsonian Magazine,* April 2003. www.smithsonianmag.com.

Anna North, "The Political and Cultural Impact of Aretha Franklin's 'Respect,' Explained," Vox, August 17, 2018. www.vox.com.

McKenzie Jean-Philippe, "40 Famous Black and African American Women Who Are Leaving Their Mark on History," Oprah Daily, January 6, 2021. www.oprahdaily.com.

Rob Sheffield, "Why Aretha Franklin Was America's Greatest Voice," *Rolling Stone,* August 17, 2018. www.rollingstone.com.

Mekeisha Madden Toby, "With 'Do the Right Thing,' Spike Lee Changed Cinema Forever," Shondaland, June 26, 2019. www.shondaland.com.

Websites
All Hip-Hip
https://allhiphop.com
This site has been covering hip-hop music and culture for more than twenty years, with videos, music streams, news, reviews, and gossip featuring the biggest and most influential rappers in the business.

40 Acres and a Mule Filmworks
https://40acres.com
This website for Spike Lee's production company features books, social media, and information about the latest films and documentaries produced by Lee and others.

Misty Copeland
https://mistycopeland.com
The official website for the first Black female principal dancer with the ABT tells the ballerina's life story, promotes ballet, provides social media links, and features performance videos and a calendar.

2Pac
www.2pac.com
This is the official website for Tupac Shakur. It contains a detailed biography, stories by those who were influenced by the rapper, and merchandise.

The Undefeated
https://theundefeated.com
This website features "The Undefeated 44," which consists of biographies of 44 influential Black American athletes, writers, musicians, politicians, and others, whose contributions changed the world.

INDEX

PICTURE CREDITS

ABOUT THE AUTHOR

Stuart A. Kallen is the author of more than 350 nonfiction books for children and young adults. He has written on topics ranging from the theory of relativity to the art of electronic dance music. In 2018 Kallen won a Green Earth Book Award from the Nature Generation environmental organization for his book *Trashing the Planet: Examining the Global Garbage Glut*. In his spare time he is a singer, songwriter, and guitarist in San Diego.